Wagner and His Dramas

Robert C. Bagar

Alpha Editions

This edition published in 2024

ISBN 9789362990273

Design and Setting By

Alpha Editions
www.alphaedis.com

Email - info@alphaedis.com

As per information held with us this book is in Public Domain. This book is a reproduction of an important historical work. Alpha Editions uses the best technology to reproduce historical work in the same manner it was first published to preserve its original nature. Any marks or number seen are left intentionally to preserve.

Contents

Foreword	- 1 -
Wagner AND HIS MUSIC-DRAMAS	- 2 -
Overture to "Rienzi"	- 11 -
Overture to "The Flying Dutchman"	- 12 -
Overture to "Tannhäuser"	- 12 -
Bacchanale from "Tannhäuser"	- 14 -
Prelude to "Lohengrin"	- 16 -
"Der Ring des Nibelungen"	- 19 -
The Ride of the Valkyries from "Die Walküre"	- 19 -
A Siegfried Idyl	- 20 -
Forest Murmurs from "Siegfried"	- 21 -
Excerpts from "Götterdämmerung"— Siegfried's Rhine Journey	- 22 -
Funeral Music	- 22 -
Brünnhilde's Immolation	- 22 -
Prelude and 'Love-Death' from "Tristan und Isolde"	- 23 -
Prelude to "Die Meistersinger von Nürnberg"	- 24 -
Excerpts from "Die Meistersinger"	- 26 -
Prelude, Transformation Scene and Grail Scene from Act 1 of "Parsifal"	- 26 -
Good Friday Spell from "Parsifal"	- 31 -

Foreword

This volume, concerned with Wagnerian excerpts most frequently performed in the concert hall, has been prepared primarily for the audience of the Philharmonic-Symphony Society of New York. Its object is to supply information in as concise and complete a manner as space will permit. It makes no boast about originality, particularly since the bulk of the material involved stems from any number of treatises on the subject of Wagner and his music.

Wagner
AND HIS MUSIC-DRAMAS

No artist has known a fiercer urge to create than Richard Wagner. None has labored more mightily to indoctrinate mankind with his convictions. None has been more scathing in his contempt of reaction, of pretense, of outdated mannerisms. He wanted his works to be sagas of epic spiritual and moral power; and, whether or not he achieved his aims, he wrote music that is voluptuous and emotionally overwhelming.

In a way he glamorized human suffering or, at least, that side of human suffering expressed through the symbol of renunciation, which one encounters frequently in his operas. His librettos are filled with super-noble purpose, with superhuman aspiration. In *Der Ring des Nibelungen* he created a world of divinities who are imperfect and humans who unconsciously strive toward perfection. It is not a new world, nor is it a brave one, except through the promise of humanity's elevation. With *Tristan und Isolde* he rises to metaphysical heights in his argument. The theme generally is again renunciation, the attaining of perfection and solace through it. One comes upon it again in *Die Meistersinger*, in *The Flying Dutchman*, in *Parsifal*, and so on.

Yet for an artist whose works so idealized all that is good and lofty and noble, Wagner did little in his own life that could possibly approach those superior motives. There is a distinction to be made, therefore, between Wagner the man and Wagner the artist.

Richard Wagner was born in Leipzig, on May 22, 1813, the son (allegedly) of Karl Friedrich and Johanna Wagner. The theory has been advanced that the composer's real father was Ludwig Geyer, an intimate friend of the family, who married Frau Wagner about a year after her first husband's death.

Madame Johanna Wagner, niece of the composer, who sang a leading role in the première performance of *Tannhäuser*.

Even as a young boy Richard was tremendously fond of the theater. His mother, not particularly interested in it, threatened to hurl a curse on his head if he attempted to make a career of the stage.

In any case, when Geyer died several years later, Richard was sent to Eisleben to become apprenticed to a goldsmith. After a year of puttering around as a tyro goldsmith he returned to Dresden where the family now was. In that city he found many opportunities to express his dramatic urge.

Soon the family moved back to Leipzig and Wagner began to study with Theodor Weinlig, who was one of the authorities on counterpoint.

His early essays in music (composition now being his aim) were nothing to become excited about. But the musical life of Dresden and his intercourse with leading figures of the day worked their influence on him nevertheless. He spent nights copying Beethoven's Fifth and Ninth Symphonies. He wrote an overture which Heinrich Dorn, director of the Leipzig Theater, liked well enough to perform, but it was poorly received. With characteristic suddenness he entered Leipzig University as a *studiosus musicae*, really a student with few privileges. But he plunged with great gusto into all sorts of student activity, which was, apparently, the real reason for his enrollment at the school.

One of his sisters, Rosalie, and his brother both followed the acting profession, and they gave him the benefit of their counsel, though no one knows how much of it he followed.

He wrote a symphony and then began work on an opera, *Die Hochzeit*, which he never completed. That was in 1832. In the same year he tried again, actually finishing a work entitled *Die Feen*. It was rejected, but Wagner, after one or two little pouts, regained his composure. He accepted an engagement as conductor at Magdeburg and in the course of his work he composed another opera, *Das Liebesverbot*, which, however, was given one performance.

At Magdeburg he met Minna Planer, a member of the operatic troupe, who later became his wife. When she left for Königsberg he followed her and obtained a conductor's position at the theater in that city. Then came a succession of changes. The restless Wagner scurried about with the spontaneity of a gypsy. When things lagged in one place he quickly moved to another. So that we find him going to Riga, where he directed both opera and symphony, to London, to Paris. In the last named he thought he might finally awaken a musical public to his genius. But he suffered untold agonies. Poverty possessed him. He and his wife lived in constant economic turmoil. With all that he managed to compose two more operas, *Rienzi* and *The Flying Dutchman*. Both were produced at Dresden under the sponsorship of Meyerbeer, then a dominant figure in German music.

All this time, though, he wrote a host of compositions, besides penning many articles on music for various publications, and his fame spread. His rebellious temperament got him into difficulty often enough, but he managed, most of the time, to slip out of it. However, in Dresden, where he officiated as a conductor of the Royal Opera, he clashed with certain musical authorities who would not brook his bold opposition to standard ideas. Yet still another opera came to the light of performance when *Tannhäuser* was given its first hearing, again at Dresden, on October 19, 1845.

During the previous summer Wagner began work on the libretto of *Die Meistersinger* while vacationing at Marienbad. He soon abandoned it, taking on the libretto for *Lohengrin* instead. The following year saw the completion of the *Lohengrin* score. In 1848 he joined a revolutionary movement that spread through Europe, launched by the French Revolution. When the disturbance was quelled some months later, he fled to Switzerland, but remained there for a short time, heading soon for Paris.

His wife refused to join him there, remembering too well the poverty of the previous stay in the French capital. But he started on *Siegfried's Death*, which was to grow into the gigantic *Ring*. He flitted about again, leaving Paris, returning a little later.

Wagner fell in love with Jessie Taylor Laussot, who proved a benefactress in a financial way. In the meantime, he decided to leave Minna forever. In Zurich, whither he repaired, he labored unceasingly on the libretto for *The Young Siegfried*. Then he created the subject of *The Valkyrie* and finally that of *The Rheingold*.

It is amusing to note that he wrote his *Ring* librettos in reverse order, that is, from what is now *Götterdämmerung* back to *Das Rheingold*. Having hit upon a huge theme, he found it increasingly necessary to broaden its scope, thus accounting for the four operas. Parenthetically, however, he wrote the music in the correct order.

The reaction of some of Wagner's musically untutored contemporaries is amusingly depicted in this caricature from *Figaro* (1876).

Wagner as a young man, about the time Meyerbeer sponsored the first production of *Rienzi* in Dresden.

Richard Wagner at the peak of his powers when *Der Ring des Nibelungen* was nearing completion.

Now in Wagner's life there appears a strange and beautiful influence, Mathilde Wesendonck, wife of a very wealthy silk merchant. It has been pointed out that under the spell of this beguiling woman his composing flourished as never before. At the home of the Wesendoncks he completed the poem for *Tristan und Isolde*. It is not known how friendly Richard and Mathilde were, but this is fact: Wagner left his friends' abode because he would not bring grief upon Otto Wesendonck.

He went once more to Paris where some very ridiculous things happened having to do with a suggested ballet for the opera

Tannhäuser. Wagner, adamant, would not change the order of his work merely to please influential gentlemen of the Jockey Club.

In 1864, when Wagner was fifty-one, he settled in Munich—he had been forgiven for his revolutionary surge—and in this musically flourishing city he came under the high patronage of King Ludwig of Bavaria. Here he renewed acquaintance with Liszt's daughter Cosima, whom he had met some years before. She was now married to Hans von Bülow, a highly gifted conductor. The composer and Cosima were thrown together a lot and their mutual regard soon ripened into love. Poor little Minna, who had been ill for a long period, died in 1866, a piece of news which saddened Wagner greatly.

That same year, however, he and Cosima took a place at Triebschen on Lake Lucerne in Switzerland. Bülow, at first angered by his wife's deed, soon came to realize the inevitability of it. Besides, he adored Wagner and his music. He acted sanely therefore, sacrificing his personal feelings for the sake of Wagner's art. Cosima and Richard were married in 1870.

At Triebschen he completed *Die Meistersinger*, *Siegfried*, and the first two acts of *Götterdämmerung*, besides writing any number of treatises, articles, and the like. Here, too, the idea of a great festival theater was born in him, and the originality of the thing soon won many influential supporters to the cause. By 1871 a site was found for it at Bayreuth, Germany. The next year he put the finishing touches to the *Ring* and the Bayreuth project grew in proportion to his frantic efforts to raise money for it. In all, it took some four years to erect this shrine to Wagnerian music. And finally, the première of the Wagnerian Cycle, running from August 13 to 16, was a tremendous success, in spite of the heartaches, the headaches, and the discouragement.

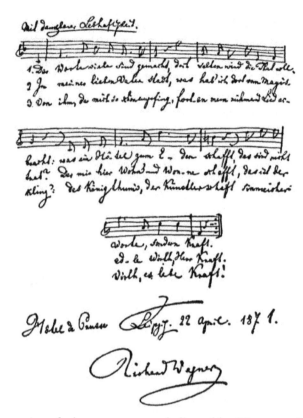

Manuscript of a humorous song dedicated by Wagner to Louis Kraft, proprietor of the hotel in Leipzig where Wagner stopped during his first trip to Bayreuth.

With all that he had already accomplished, Wagner could have retired to the easy life he often so fervently spoke about. But the urge to compose never left him. He set to work on *Parsifal*, the poem he had completed some months before. When the opera was all finished he endeavored with his usual kinetic energy to raise money for its production. It was given its first performance on July 26, 1882. There were sixteen more performances.

Wagner, after all the excitement of Bayreuth, left for a vacation in Venice. In spite of repeated heart attacks, he considered seriously the writing of another symphony. But he had done his work. There was to be no second symphony. Wagner died of his heart illness on February 13, 1883. He was buried at Bayreuth.

Overture to "Rienzi"

Bulwer's *Rienzi* revived an old desire of Wagner's to make an opera out of the story of the last of the Tribunes. He was in Dresden during the summer of 1837 and there he read Barmann's translation of the Bulwer novel. However, he did not begin actual work until the following July. First, of course, came the text. Later that month he started on the music. By May 1839, he had completed two acts. The remainder of the score, with the exception of the Overture, was written and orchestrated in Paris. The Overture was finished on October 23, 1840.

On October 20, 1842, *Rienzi* was given its world première at the Royal Saxon Court Theater, Dresden. Amusingly, the performance began at 6 P.M., and it went on and on until midnight. America was not to become acquainted with the opera until March 4, 1878, when it was given at the Academy of Music, New York.

The thematic material employed in the Overture stems from music in the opera itself, such as the "long-sustained, swelled and diminished A on the trumpet," which is the signal for the people's uprising against the nobles; Rienzi's Prayer; a theme of the chorus, *Gegrüsst sei hoher Tag*; the theme of the revolutionary forces, *Santo spirito cavaliere*; the stretto of the second Finale, *Rienzi, dir sei Preis*; and a subject similar to the phrase of the nobles set to the words, *Ha, dieser Gnade Schmach erdruckt das stolze Herz!*

The score of the Overture calls for one piccolo, two flutes, two oboes, two clarinets, two bassoons, two valve-horns, two plain horns, one serpent (nowadays replaced by the double-bassoon), two valve trumpets, two plain trumpets, three trombones, one ophicleide (replaced by the bass-tuba), two snare-drums, bass drum, triangle, cymbals, and strings.

The People's Chorus, commencing Act II of *Rienzi*.

OVERTURE TO "THE FLYING DUTCHMAN"

This compact and brilliantly written Overture calls for the following instrumentation: piccolo, two flutes, two oboes, English horn, two clarinets, four horns, two bassoons, two trumpets, three trombones, bass tuba, kettledrums, harp, and strings.

John Runciman once remarked about this music, "It is the atmosphere of the sea that counts; the roar of the billows, the 'hui!' of the wind, the dashing and plunging.... The sea, indeed, is the background, foreground, the whole environment of the drama.... The smell and atmosphere of the sea is maintained with extraordinary vividness to the last bar."

In the construction of the Overture Wagner makes important use of the theme of the Dutchman, which appears in the opening measure by horns and bassoons, and of the up-and-down theme of Senta, the Angel of Mercy, softly and tenderly sung by English horn, horns and bassoons. This is the theme which at the conclusion of the piece rises to a triumphant sonority, indicative of redemption attained.

OVERTURE TO "TANNHÄUSER"

The first concert performance of this well-known Overture took place at Leipzig, on February 12, 1846, under the direction of Mendelssohn. The event was a benefit for the Gewandhaus Orchestra Pension Fund.

Wagner himself furnished a "program" for the Overture when the musicians performing it at a Zurich concert requested an explanation of the music. The "program" in a translation by William Ashton Ellis follows:

"To begin with, the orchestra leads before us the Pilgrim's Chorus alone; it draws near, then swells into a mighty outpour, and passes finally away.—Evenfall; last echo of the chant. As night breaks, magic sights and sounds appear, a rosy mist floats up, exultant shouts assail our ears, the whirlings of a fearsomely voluptuous dance are seen. These are the Venusberg's seductive spells, that show themselves at dead of night to those whose breast is fired by the daring of the senses. Attracted by the tempting show, a shapely human form draws nigh; 'tis Tannhäuser, Love's minstrel.... Venus herself appears to him.... As the Pilgrim's Chant draws closer, yet closer, as the day drives farther back the night, that whir and soughing of the air—which had erewhile sounded like the eerie cries of the soul condemned—now rises, too, to ever gladder waves; so that when the sun ascends at last in splendor, and the Pilgrims' Chant proclaims in ecstasy to all the world, to all that lives and moves thereon, Salvation won, this wave itself swells out the tidings of sublimest joy. 'Tis the carol of the Venusberg itself, redeemed from the curse of impiousness, this cry we hear amid the hymn of God. So wells and leaps each pulse of Life in chorus of Redemption; and both dissevered elements, both soul and senses, God and Nature, unite in the astonishing kiss of hallowed Love."

TANNHAUSER
"Wagner, inventor of the bass drum for musical bombardment, applies himself to his favorite exercise" reads the caption for this contemporary French caricature.

The Overture to Tannhäuser is scored for piccolo, two flutes, two oboes, two clarinets, two bassoons, four horns, three trumpets, three trombones, bass tuba, kettledrums, cymbals, triangle, tambourine, and strings.

BACCHANALE FROM "TANNHÄUSER"

The opera was first produced at the Royal Opera House, Dresden, on October 19, 1845. Some sixteen years later, due to the interest and influence of Princess Metternich, wife of the Austrian Ambassador to France, the work was introduced to Paris. For that production Wagner extended his first scene to include a Bacchanale, the reasons for this being as amusing to us as they must have been tragic to Wagner. The Princess revealed, in an article written for the *Pall Mall Magazine* (London, 1894) some of the reasons for the failure of the opera there, and it was a complete failure. The Princess says:

"The day of the performance drew nigh and in most circles little good will was confessed. It was stated generally that a protest should be made against the abominable futurist music, and it was rumored that stormy scenes might be expected at the Opera. In the clubs men were annoyed because Wagner would not have a regular ballet, but only a few poses of the ballerinas in the Venusberg. The club subscribers to the Opera expected a ballet at nine-thirty sharp, no matter what the opera. This, at least, was the custom of the time. No one who knew anything of art could conceive where a ballet could be introduced into the midst of 'Tannhäuser.' Wagner declared that he would not accede to the silly wishes of the subscribers, because he could not. And he was perfectly right, but his refusal was to be paid for dearly."

Wagner had entertained great hopes for this Parisian production of *Tannhäuser*. To produce his work at the justly famed Opera was reason enough, what with that organization's habit of letting expense go hang. He labored industriously at making revisions, which included a complete rewrite of the Bacchanalian scene as well as of the music for Venus and Tannhäuser in Act 1.

When he had completed his revisions he played the music for several friends. Charles Nuitter, one of these, reported on that private hearing as follows:

"When we arrived the composer sat down to the piano. He played with indescribable animation and fury. His hands pounded the keys, and the same time he strove to acquaint me with the action of the scene, crying out the entrance of the various groups. 'Arrival of the fauns and satyrs; all are put to flight; the confusion mounts to its climax,' he flung at me, and his hands continued to bang the keys, the musical delirium always augmenting. When he was piling on a succession of quivering chords Wagner suddenly cried, 'Now a crash of thunder. We are all dead!' At that moment a wagon of paving stones discharged its load into the street, thus producing a prolonged and terrible noise. Wagner turned round and regarded us with stupefaction, his eyes staring wildly. It took us some moments to recover from this stirring of our feelings. Thus it was that I was initiated into the new music."

The first Paris performance of *Tannhäuser* took place on March 13, 1861. That was the first of three fiascos in the French capital. The second occurred on March 18. Napoleon III and the Empress both attended, but their presence had no effect on the rest of the audience, whose cat-calls, howls, and kindred strange noises were even louder, if not funnier, than the first time.

The work was given for the third time on March 24. This was not a regular subscription performance, and it seemed to all and sundry that finally a Parisian audience would be honest and unprejudiced in its attitude toward the opera. However, the composer's enemies had bought out the house and the result was the same. Whereupon Wagner withdrew his score. *Tannhäuser* was not given again in Paris until thirty-four years later.

Prelude to "Lohengrin"

In the summer of 1845, while Wagner was at Marienbad, he worked out the plan for *Lohengrin*. The libretto he wrote during the following winter. Then came a topsy-turvy scheme of creation. In composing the music he began with the hero's Narrative in the last act, "because the monologue contained the most significant musical germs in the whole score." He finished the third act on March 25, 1847, the first act on June 8 of that year, the second act on August 2, and the Prelude on August 28. The orchestration was done during the following winter and spring. Franz Liszt conducted the première of the opera at Weimar on August 28, 1850. The Prelude was played for the first time in concert on January 17, 1853, at the Leipzig Gewandhaus, Julius Rietz conducting.

Discussing the Prelude, William Foster Apthorp wrote:

"Like the hero's career in the opera, it begins, as it were, in the clouds, then gradually descends farther and farther until it embraces all the lower tones of the orchestra, and then returns to the clouds again. Its single theme is developed in free polyphony by various successive groups of instruments, each of which groups proceeds with free counter-thematic work as the next group enters with the theme. First we have the violins *piano* in their higher registers; then come the flutes, oboes, and clarinets; then the violas, 'cellos, horns, bassoons, and double-basses; lastly the trumpets, trombones, and the tuba *fortissimo*;

then comes the *decrescendo*, ending *pianissimo* in the high violins and flutes."

The composer, who could descant with the best of them, paraded his rhetorical gifts on the Prelude (the translation is by William Ashton Ellis):

"Love seemed to have vanished from a world of hatred and quarreling; as a lawgiver she was no longer to be found among the communities of men. Emancipating itself from barren care for gain and possession, the sole arbiter of all worldly intercourse, the human heart's unquenchable love-longing, again at length craved to appease a want which, the more warmly and intensely it made itself felt under the pressure of reality, was the less easy to satisfy on account of this very reality. It was beyond the confines of the actual world that man's ecstatic imaginative power fixed the source as well as the output of this incomprehensible impulse of love, and from the desire of a comforting sensuous conception of this supersensuous idea invested it with a wonderful form, which, under the name of the 'Holy Grail,' though conceived as actually existing, yet unapproachably far off, was believed in, longed for, and sought for.

"The Holy Grail was the costly vessel out of which, at the Last Supper, our Saviour drank with His disciples, and in which His blood was received when out of love for His brethren He suffered upon the cross, and which till this day has been preserved with lively zeal as the source of undying love; albeit, at one time this cup of salvation was taken away from unworthy mankind, but at length was brought back again from the heights of heaven by a band of angels, and delivered into the keeping of fervently loving, solitary men who, wondrously strengthened and blessed by its presence, and purified in heart, were consecrated as the earthly champions of eternal love.

"This miraculous delivery of the Holy Grail, escorted by an angelic host, and the handing of it over into the custody of highly favored men, was selected by the author of 'Lohengrin' for the introduction of his drama, as the subject to be musically portrayed; just as here, for the sake of explanation, he may be allowed to bring it forward as an object for the mental receptive power of his hearers.

"To the enraptured look of the highest celestial longing for love, the clearest blue atmosphere of heaven at first seems to condense itself into a wonderful, scarcely perceptible but magically pleasing vision; with gradually increasing precision the wonder-working angelic host is delineated in infinitely delicate lines as, conveying the holy vessel (the Grail) in its midst, it insensibly descends from the blazing heights of heaven. As the vision grows more and more distinct, as it hovers over the surface of the earth, a narcotic fragrant odor issues from its midst; entrancing vapors well up from it like golden clouds, and overpower the sense of the astonished gazer, who, from the lowest depths of his palpitating heart, feels himself wonderfully urged to holy emotions.

"Now throbs the heart with the pain of ecstasy, now with the heavenly joy which agitates the breast of the beholder; with irresistible might all the repressed germs of love rise up in it, stimulated to a wondrous growth by the vivifying magic of the vision; however much it can expand, it will break at last with vehement longing, impelled to self-sacrifice and toward an ultimate dissolving reveals again in the supremest bliss as, imparting comfort the nearer it approaches, the divine vision reveals itself to our entranced senses, and when at last the holy vessel shows itself in the marvel of undraped reality, and clearly revealed to him to whom it is vouchsafed to behold it, as the Holy Grail, which from out of its divine contents spreads broadcast the sunbeams of highest love, like the lights of a heavenly fire that stirs all hearts with the heat of the flame of its everlasting glow, the beholder's brain reels—he falls down in a state of adoring annihilation. Yet upon him who is thus lost in love's rapture the Grail pours down its blessing, with which it designates him as its chosen knight; the blazing flame subsides into an ever-decreasing brightness, which now, like a gasp of breath of the most unspeakable joy and emotion, spreads itself over the surface of the earth and fills the breast of him who adores with a blessedness of which he had no foreboding. With chaste rejoicing, and smilingly looking down, the angelic host mounts again to heaven's heights; the source of love, which had dried up the earth, has been brought by them to the world again—the Grail they have left in the custody of the pure-minded men, in whose hands its contents overflow as a source of blessing—and the angelic host vanishes in the glorious light of heaven's blue sky, as, before, it thence came down."

"DER RING DES NIBELUNGEN"

A colossal work in four parts, the *Ring's* central theme is one of redemption. The Norse God Wotan, addicted to the amassing of power, may not achieve it through deceit or treachery. By trickery he obtains from the Nibelung Alberich a ring possessing untold powers, made of the gold of the Rhine. Alberich hisses a curse, in losing it, which only a pure hero acting as a free agent may remove.

Wotan's attempts to get the ring, his often devious reasoning, and the panoplied purpose of the whole, make of the tetralogy an epic study in the emotions, the humanities, the loyalties, the shortcomings, in short, in the whole moral and spiritual concept of the individual and society.

THE RIDE OF THE VALKYRIES FROM "DIE WALKÜRE"

In the time intervening between *Das Rheingold* and *Die Walküre* Wotan has worked out a plan to save the gods from destruction. The ring must not fall into the wrong hands, those of Alberich, for instance, for the wily and greedy creature knows full well its powers. The thing to do, then, is to regain possession of it without "craft or violence." He must employ some means above such devices. Consequently his plan is to bring into being a hero who shall not be his servitor, but rather the agency for the accomplishment through a free, totally unguided will. Thus we come to the saga of the Walsungs, human descendants of Wotan, and one of them, Siegmund, is the hero chosen.

The Valkyries are the nine daughters of Wotan by the earth goddess of wisdom, Erda. And of these Brünnhilde is Wotan's favorite. She interferes with her father's wishes in order to aid Siegmund, however, and she is given the penalty of mortality by her father. The duet in the last act of the opera between Wotan and Brünnhilde is one of the most moving sequences in all Wagner.

The Ride of the Valkyries is an excerpt from the music which leads into Act III, made into a concert piece by Wagner himself. A great rock dominates the scene in the opera. It is the Valkyr Rock where now the maidens are gathering. Fully equipped in shining mail, carrying spears and shields, they ride swiftly through the storm. At the curtain's rise only four of the maidens are discernible on the stage. The others may be heard announcing their entrance with the exultant Valkyr call. The music surges to great heights of sound, wild, untrammeled, passionate, driven relentlessly by powerful rhythms.

A SIEGFRIED IDYL

In a letter dated June 25, 1870, Wagner wrote of his wife Cosima, "She has defied every disapprobation and taken upon herself every condemnation. She has borne to me a wonderfully beautiful boy, whom I call boldly Siegfried; he is now growing, together with my work [he was working then on the opera *Siegfried*; hence the name]; he gives me a new long life, which at last has attained a meaning. Thus we get along without the world, from which we have wholly withdrawn."

The composer wrote the music of the *Idyl*—originally called the *Triebschen Idyl*—as a birthday gift for his wife. On Christmas morning, 1870, Wagner and a group of musicians assembled on the stairs of his home at Triebschen and performed the lovely music, which, cramped though the musicians were because of tight quarters, obtained a fine rendering, according to ear-witnesses.

When the *Idyl* was first played in Berlin, in 1878, a music critic gave it as gospel that the music was taken from the second act of the opera *Siegfried*. The truth of the matter is that the *Idyl*, while based on several themes from the opera besides that of a folk song, is a complete entity in itself, for the themes were developed in a manner entirely different from their treatment in the opera. In addition to which, it must be remembered that the folk song, *Schlaf, mein Kind, schlaf'ein*, does not appear in the opera at all.

"Wagner and the Critics" is the title of this amusing contemporary caricature.

FOREST MURMURS FROM "SIEGFRIED"

The music for this sequence is taken from the scene before the dragon's cave in the second act of *Siegfried*. In arranging it for concert use, Wagner gave it the name *Waldweben* (*Forest Weavings* or *Forest Murmurs*). The young hero Siegfried is left to his own thoughts by the dwarf Mime. The rustling of the leaves is first heard in D minor, then in B major. Siegfried is daydreaming. He ponders on the question of his origin. He knows that he is not of Mime's blood, and the clarinet, paralleling, and explaining the idea, intones the theme of the Volsungs.

As his thoughts turn to his mother the Love-Life motive emerges through the 'cellos and violas and double basses, next in all the strings, and finally horns and bassoons take it over. A solo violin plays a subject associated with Freia, goddess of youth and love. The rustling of the leaves is again heard and the theme of the Forest Bird comes in by way of the oboe, flute, clarinet and other wood winds. The music ends in a Vivace which incorporates the Fire, the Siegfried, and the Slumber motives, besides the twittering of the Forest Bird.

Excerpts from "Götterdämmerung"—Siegfried's Rhine Journey

This music comes between the Prologue and the first act. It is frequently referred to as a "scherzo." Siegfried has taken leave of his wife Brünnhilde and, exhorted by her, sallies forth on new adventures. The music brings up the hero's past achievements, whose themes are presented in new guises. They are cleverly interwoven, the pattern being rich in colors and effects as well as in sonorities. Through the orchestral web may be detected threads akin to such thematic ideas as Siegfried's horn call, the Rhine motive, the motive of Renunciation, the motive of the Rhine Daughters, the motive of the Rheingold and, last, that of the Nibelungs' Servitude. Climactic and exultant, the music yet gives forth many implications of impending tragedy.

Funeral Music

Through the trickery of Hagen, villainous half-brother of Gunther, Siegfried is slain. His body is lifted tenderly by Gunther's followers and carried back to the hall of the Gibichungs. As that happens on the stage, the orchestra sings out with a giant dirge, lamenting the fall of the Volsungs while reviewing previous moments in the history of the tragic race. There is the reference to the love of Siegmund and Sieglinde from *Die Walküre*. Toward its conclusion the horns and bass trumpet announce sonorously the motive of Siegfried the hero. There is a rhythmic variant of the horn call and with the dying away of the music Brünnhilde is momentarily mentioned.

Brünnhilde's Immolation

The end of the gigantic *Ring*, specifically Brünnhilde's scene of immolation, is frequently performed in concert with a soprano soloist. The heroine's great monologue, delivered in the hall of the Gibichungs, writes finis to a drama that takes four separate operas to tell. In her grief over the death of her hero-husband she stills the "loud, unworthy" lamentations of the others who are gathered about the slain Siegfried. She commands them to erect a funeral pyre and to place the hero's body upon it. His ring is taken from his finger and she puts it on her own. After applying a torch to the pyre she leaps on her horse Grane and rushes into the flames.

PRELUDE AND 'LOVE-DEATH' FROM "TRISTAN UND ISOLDE"

In 1854, when Wagner was in the midst of composing the *Ring*, the idea for an opera on the Tristan theme came to him. Not till three years later, however, did he begin actual work on it, and the music-drama was finished in August 1859. Complications of various kinds interfered with the production of the opera, but it finally obtained its première at the Royal Court Theater in Munich, on June 10, 1865, under the direction of Hans von Bülow.

Wagner's version of the tale combines features from numerous legends. Very likely of Celtic origin, the story, as the German composer utilized it, makes room for myriad delvings into psychology and metaphysics, some of which are not easy to follow. We must assume, as Ernest Newman suggests, that the characters and their motivations were perfectly clear to the composer, if they seem not to be altogether to the listener. Here is the essence of the music-drama's plot, extracted from Wagner's own description:

We are told of Tristan and Isolde in an ancient love poem, which is "constantly fashioning itself anew, and has been adopted by every European language of the Middle Ages." Tristan, a faithful vassal of King Marke, woos Isolde for his king, yet not daring to reveal to her his own love. "Isolde, powerless to do otherwise, follows him as a bride to his lord." In the meantime the Goddess of Love, balked by all this, plans revenge. The Love Potion, which had been intended for the king in order to insure the marriage, is given to Tristan and Isolde to drink, a circumstance which "... opens their eyes to the truth and leads to the avowal that for the future they belong only to each other.... The world, power, fame, splendor, honor, knighthood, fidelity, friendship, all are dissipated like an empty dream. One thing only remains: longing, longing, insatiable longing, forever springing up anew, pining and thirsting. Death, which means passing away, perishing, never awakening, their only deliverance.... Shall we call it death? Or is it the hidden wonder-world from out of which an ivy and vine, entwined with each other, grew upon Tristan's and Isolde's grave, as the legend tells us?"

The Prelude, A minor, 6-8, makes a very gradual and long *crescendo* to a mighty *fortissimo*, followed by a briefer *decrescendo*, which leads to a whispered *pianissimo*. Free as to form and ever widening in scope of development, it offers two chief themes: a phrase, uttered by the 'cellos, is united to another, given to the oboes, to form a subject called the "Love Potion" theme, or the theme of "Longing." Another theme, again announced by the 'cellos, "Tristan's Love Glance," is sensuous, even voluptuous in character.

After the Prelude, the orchestra enters into the "Liebestod" or "Love-Death," that passionate flow of phrases, taken mostly from the material in the second act Love-Duet. Isolde (in the opera) sings her song of sublimated desire. Franz Liszt is responsible for the application of the term "Liebestod" to that part of the music which originally had been named "Verklärung" by Wagner himself.

PRELUDE TO "DIE MEISTERSINGER VON NÜRNBERG"

"The completion of *Die Meistersinger*, Triebschen, Thursday, October 24, 1867, 8 o'clock in the evening, R. W." These words were inscribed on the last sheet of the manuscript of Wagner's only operatic comedy. This was some twenty-two years after the very first drafts were drawn at Marienbad. The doctor had ordered a complete rest. But rest to Wagner meant ennui. Perhaps, he thought, he might be able to rest while composing a lighter work. The idea took hold. He gave it considerable thought. He could just about see this airy piece's "rapid circulation through the European opera houses." Indeed, he judged that "something thoroughly light and popular" might be just the thing to make his everlasting fame.

Hans Sachs, of course, is the hero of this masterpiece. A historic character, Sachs was built by the composer into something of an ideal of homespun charm and wit and philosophy. But Wagner also evened a score with an old enemy in his composition of this work. The music critic Eduard Hanslick appears as the crotchety, pedantic and unprincipled Beckmesser, thus earning for himself a ridiculous immortality.

How Wagner could have written this opera with all the troubles besetting him is hard to comprehend. Yet no financial snarls, domestic tribulations, romantic attachments or what-not could stay it even though it took years to come forth.

As for the Prelude, Wagner himself has written an interesting analysis, which is here appended:

"The opening theme for the 'cellos has already been heard in the third strophe of Sachs' cobbler-song in Act II. There is expressed the bitter cry of the man who has determined to renounce his personal happiness, yet who shows the world a cheerful, resolute exterior. That smothered cry was understood by Eva, and so deeply did it pierce her heart that she fain would fly away, if only to hear this cheerful-seeming song no longer. Now, in the Introduction to Act III, this motive is played alone by the 'cellos, and developed in the other strings till it dies away in resignation; but forthwith, and as from out the distance, the horns intone the solemn song wherewith Hans Sachs greeted Luther and the Reformation, which had won the poet such incomparable popularity. After the first strophe the strings again take single phrases of the cobbler's song, very softly and much slower, as though the man were turning his gaze from his handiwork heavenwards, and lost in tender musings. Then, with increased sonority, the horns pursue the master's hymn, with which Hans Sachs, at the end of the act, is greeted by the populace of Nuremberg. Next reappears the strings' first motive, with grandiose expression of the anguish of a deeply-stirred soul; calmed and allayed, it attains the utmost serenity of a blest and peaceful resignation."

The plot of *Die Meistersinger* deals with a song contest which is to be held in Nuremberg on St. John's Day. Naturally, there is to be a handsome prize for the winner and in this case it is the hand of Eva, daughter of the goldsmith Veit Pogner. A young knight, Walther von Stolzing, has seen Eva meanwhile, and he has fallen in love with her. Because he is a likeable young man, he is given permission to enter the contest. Another contestant is Beckmesser, the town clerk, who attempts to bring Walther to ruin.

However, Walther and Eva have confessed their love for each other to Hans Sachs, a cobbler, who happens also to be in love with Eva. But he makes the supreme sacrifice, rejoicing at the same time in the knowledge that the maid will be deliriously happy with her young knight. He helps their cause along, writing down the notes of a song Walther has heard in a dream. At the contest Beckmesser tries to sing that same song, offering it as his own, but his raucous efforts make him the laughing stock of the affair. Of course, Walther's song is adjudged the best and he wins his Eva.

EXCERPTS FROM "DIE MEISTERSINGER"

Often heard in the concert hall are several other excerpts from *Die Meistersinger*. These include the Procession of the Guilds, the Dance of the Apprentices, the Procession of the Masters, the Homage to Sachs, and the Finale.

PRELUDE, TRANSFORMATION SCENE AND GRAIL SCENE FROM ACT 1 OF "PARSIFAL"

Most of the *Ring*, all of *Tristan*, and a considerable portion of *Die Meistersinger* had been written by Wagner before he started actual work on the "consecrational festival stage play," *Parsifal*, in 1865. He made a first outline of the libretto in August of that year, some two decades after he had become acquainted with the Parsifal poem of Wolfram von Eschenbach, the Minnesinger. Not till 1877, however, did the text attain its final shape, and it was published in December. Sometime previously Wagner had turned to the task of composing the music and completed it in 1879. The orchestration was finished in January 1882. The opera was given for the first time at Bayreuth on July 26, 1882. The Prelude, written in December 1878, had been given its première performance at Wagner's house, Wahnfried, on Christmas Day, with the composer conducting for the occasion, his wife Cosima's birthday.

Wagner with Franz Liszt and Liszt's daughter, Cosima, ex-wife of the conductor Hans von Bülow, whom Wagner married in 1870.

The Wagner villa, *Wahnfried*, at Bayreuth, scene of the Wagnerian Festivals.
Publisher's Photo Service

The ethical essence of *Parsifal* has thus been expressed: "Enlightenment coming through conscious pity brings salvation." Wagner, whose earlier music-dramas each revolved about some *idée fixe* of philosophical or moral implication, brought to *Parsifal*, besides, religious elements derived from the twin sources of Christian doctrine and Buddhism. Some years before he had done the sketch for a play on the subject of Jesus of Nazareth, and, parenthetically, it is quite likely that he had no intention to write music for it. Nevertheless, here is shown the composer's religious urge, mingled with other aspects of his creative bent. He says, "I was burning to write something that should take the message of my tortured brain, and speak in a fashion to be understood by present life. Just as with my Siegfried, the force of my desire had borne me to the fount of the Eternal Human: so now, when I found this desire cut off by modern life from all appeasement, and saw afresh that the sole redemption lay in flight from out this life, casting off its claims on me by self-destruction, did I come to the fount of every modern rendering of such a situation—Jesus of Nazareth, the Man."

During that period Wagner drafted another play, which he titled *Die Seger (The Victors)*, one of Buddhistic import, whose story centers on the dictum that Prakriti, the hero, may not become one with Amanda, the heroine, unless he "shares the latter's vow of chastity." In these two works may be found qualities and tones of thought also incorporated in *Parsifal*.

The locale of *Parsifal* is Montsalvat in the Spanish Pyrenees. The castle of the Holy Grail is tenanted by a company of Knights, guardians of the Spear which pierced Jesus' side as He hung on the Cross, and of the Cup He drank from the Last Supper and which received His precious blood from the Spear-wound. This brotherhood of Knights of the Grail refuses membership to all, save the pure in heart, and the Knights go about the world doing good through the high powers given them by the Grail.

A certain other knight, Klingsor, sinful and scheming, enraged against the Knights for having been denied admission to the Brotherhood, has built a magic garden, whose many charms have proved strong enough to tempt several of the weaker-willed Knights. Amfortas, king of the Grail, is one of these. He has fallen victim to the wiles of Kundry, a creature of Klingsor. The latter has seized the Spear from Amfortas and has humiliated him further by wounding him with it. The wound may be cured only by being touched with the point of the Spear held by a Guileless Fool, a youth who can withstand all temptation. This youth, of course, is Parsifal, a forest lad who enters into the picture through having killed a swan sacred to the Grail. Parsifal is made to go through the rituals prescribed by the libretto; namely, he is present at the ceremony of the Eucharist or the Lord's Supper without grasping anything of its meaning; he resists the lures thriving in Klingsor's garden; then he seizes the Spear, flung at him by Klingsor and, as he makes the sign of the cross, the garden is destroyed. He wanders about the world and returns to Montsalvat. Kundry, now a repentant woman dedicated to the Grail's service, washes his feet and dries them with her hair. Next he goes with Gurnemanz to the temple where he restores Amfortas to health, and, as the latter bends before him in homage, Kundry dies. Having thus attained "enlightenment ... through conscious pity," Parsifal has become the saviour of Montsalvat.

The Prelude is an abbreviated exposition of the purposes, musical and dramatic, of the opera. It opens with the phrase which dominates the religious scene of the first act during the feast of the Lord's Supper. The phrase, sung first in unison by violins, 'cellos, English horn, clarinet and bassoons, is marked *sehr langsam* (Lento assai), A-flat major, 4-4. It is taken up by trumpet, oboes, and half the first and second violins to the accompaniment of arpeggios in the violas and the other violins, and chords for flutes, clarinets, and English horn with the bassoons and horns sustaining harmony notes. After a series of broken chords, the trombones and trumpets announce a second theme, the Grail motive, which is a phrase long known as the *Dresden Amen* of the Saxon liturgy. There is a change of tempo to 6-4 with the entrance of a third theme, that of Faith. Its first figure is frequently repeated against changing harmonies. A fourth theme appears, suggestive of the suffering of Christ and Amfortas, which originates in the Lord's Supper motive; its first two measures are also employed to characterize the Spear. In the words of Maurice Kufferath, "Like the Prelude to 'Lohengrin,' the introduction to 'Parsifal' is developed by successive degrees until it reaches a maximum of expression, thereafter to diminish imperceptibly to a pianissimo. Thus the synthesis of the whole drama is clearly exposed. That which remains is merely a peroration, a logical, necessary conclusion brought about by the ideas associated with the different themes."

The music of the Transformation Scene in this act is that which is played during the walk of the venerable Gurnemanz and

Parsifal through the wood to the Hall of the Grail. The music is of a march-like quality for a spell, subsequently gradually expanding in color and richness to the climactic theme representative of the Penitence of Amfortas, which is given out three times in succession.

The Grail Scene follows. There is the tolling of bells, the Grail Knights march into the hall in stately fashion. One hears the chanting of boys in the lofty dome. The ritual is interrupted by the impassioned song of Amfortas, who, suffering great torment, begs his father, Titurel, in words of self-abasement, to celebrate the Communion in his place. Titurel answers, however, "Serve thou, and so thy guilt atone! Uncover the Grail!" Presently the ceremony is ended, the knights have departed, and only Gurnemanz and Parsifal remain. The former inquires of the latter how much of the proceedings he has understood. The youth's only answer is to clutch at his heart and shake his head. Gurnemanz, who by this time is convinced that Parsifal is truly a fool, sends him away angrily and then follows the Knights out the door. From somewhere above an unseen singer delivers the motive of the Pure Fool. The theme of the Grail is sung by still other voices. Bells peal once again. The act ends.

Rough draft of one of Wagner's last compositions, dedicated to his wife, Cosima.

It is interesting to note that these excerpts from *Parsifal* represent the only ones authorized by Wagner for concert performance.

GOOD FRIDAY SPELL FROM "PARSIFAL"

The Good Friday Spell is placed at the end of the first scene in Act III of the opera. Gurnemanz is now an old hermit who lives in a humble abode at the edge of a forest. He comes out of the hut when he hears a groaning sound in the distance. Presently Parsifal arrives. He is a knight clad in black armor, carrying the sacred spear and a buckler. He is weary. The old Gurnemanz plies him with questions, but Parsifal will not answer until he is apprised of the fact that it is Good Friday. Whereupon he drives the spear into the ground, removes his helmet, and kneels in prayer.

Subsequently Kundry fetches water and washes his feet and anoints him with holy oil. And Gurnemanz, recognizing in him the Guileless Fool now worthy of the title King of the Grail, blesses him and greets him as the king. They soon set out for Montsalvat.

The music of the Good Friday Spell comprises thematically a hymn of thanksgiving, the music of Kundry's Sigh, of the Holy Supper, of the Spear, of the Grail, of the Complaint, of the Flower Girls. All of these are finally fused into a pastoral poem ending with the Good Friday melody, which is suddenly interrupted by the doleful sound of bells. During Gurnemanz's blessing of Parsifal, horns, trumpets and trombones play the Parsifal motive. This is given out in an impressive manner, and it leads into the Grail theme. There follows a series of chords which usher in the motives of Baptism and Faith.

COMPLETE LIST OF RECORDINGS BY THE PHILHARMONIC-SYMPHONY SOCIETY OF NEW YORK

COLUMBIA RECORDS

LP—Also available on Long Playing Microgroove Recordings as well as on the conventional Columbia Masterworks.

Under the Direction of Bruno Walter

BARBER—Symphony No. 1, Op. 9

BEETHOVEN—Concerto for Violin, Cello, Piano and Orchestra in C major (with J. Corigliano, L. Rose and W. Hendl)—LP

BEETHOVEN—Concerto No. 5 in E-flat major ("Emperor") (with Rudolf Serkin, piano)—LP

BEETHOVEN—Concerto in D major for Violin and Orchestra (with Joseph Szigeti)—LP

BEETHOVEN—Symphony No. 1 in C major, Op. 21—LP

BEETHOVEN—Symphony No. 3 in E-flat major ("Eroica")—LP

BEETHOVEN—Symphony No. 5 in C minor—LP

BEETHOVEN—Symphony No. 8 in F major—LP

BEETHOVEN—Symphony No. 9 in D minor ("Choral") (with Elena Nikolaidi, contralto, and Raoul Jobin, tenor)—LP

BRAHMS—Song of Destiny (with Westminster Choir)—LP

DVORAK—Slavonic Dance No. 1

DVORAK—Symphony No. 4 in G Major—LP

MAHLER—Symphony No. 4 in G major (with Desi Halban, soprano)—LP

MAHLER—Symphony No. 5 in C-sharp minor

MENDELSSOHN—Concerto in E minor (with Nathan Milstein, violin)—LP

MENDELSSOHN—Scherzo (from Midsummer Night's Dream)

MOZART—Cosi fan Tutti—Overture

MOZART—Symphony No. 41 in C major ("Jupiter"), K. 551—LP

SCHUBERT—Symphony No. 7 in C major—LP

SCHUMANN, R.—Symphony No. 3 in E-flat major ("Rhenish")—LP

SMETANA—The Moldau ("Vltava")—LP

STRAUSS, J.—Emperor Waltz

Under the Direction of Leopold Stokowski

COPLAND—Billy the Kid (2 parts)

GRIFFES—"The White Peacock," Op. 7, No. 1—LP 7"

IPPOLITOW—"In the Village" from Caucasian Sketches (W. Lincer and M. Nazzi, soloists)

KHACHATURIAN—"Masquerade Suite"—LP

MESSIAN—"L'Ascension"—LP

SIBELIUS—"Maiden with the Roses"—LP

TSCHAIKOWSKY—Francesca da Rimini, Op. 32—LP

TSCHAIKOWSKY—Overture Fantasy—Romeo and Juliet—LP

VAUGHAN-WILLIAMS—Greensleeves

VAUGHAN-WILLIAMS—Symphony No. 6 in E minor—LP

WAGNER—Die Walküre—Wotan Farewell and Magic Fire Music (Act III—Scene 3)

WAGNER—Siegfried's Rhine journey and Siegfried's Funeral March—("Die Götterdämmerung")—LP

Under the Direction of Efrem Kurtz

CHOPIN—Les Sylphides—LP

GLINKA—Mazurka—"Life of the Czar"—LP 7"

GRIEG—Concerto in A minor for Piano and Orchestra, Op. 16 (with Oscar Levant, piano)—LP

HEROLD—Zampa—Overture

KABALEVSKY—"The Comedians," Op. 26—LP

KHACHATURIAN—Gayne—Ballet Suite No. 1—LP

KHACHATURIAN—Gayne—Ballet Suite No. 2—LP

LECOQ—Mme. Angot Suite—LP

PROKOFIEFF—March, Op. 99—LP

RIMSKY-KORSAKOV—The Flight of the Bumble Bee—LP 7"

SHOSTAKOVICH—Polka No. 3, "The Age of Gold"—LP 7"

SHOSTAKOVICH—Symphony No. 9—LP

SHOSTAKOVICH—Valse from "Les Monts D'Or"—LP

VILLA-LOBOS—Uirapuru—LP

WIENIAWSKI—Concerto No. 2 in D minor for Violin and Orchestra, Op. 22 (with Isaac Stern, violin)—LP

Under the Direction of Charles Münch

D'INDY—Symphony on a French Mountain Air for Orchestra and Piano—LP

MILHAUD—Suite Française—LP

MOZART—Concerto No. 21 for Piano and Orchestra in C major—LP

SAINT-SAENS—Symphony In C minor, No. 3 for Orchestra, Organ and Piano, Op. 78—LP

Under the Direction of Artur Rodzinski

BIZET—Carmen—Entr'acte (Prelude to Act III)

BIZET—Symphony in C major—LP

BRAHMS—Symphony No. 1 in C minor—LP

BRAHMS—Symphony No. 2 in D major—LP

COPLAND—A Lincoln Portrait (with Kenneth Spencer, Narrator)—LP

ENESCO—Roumanian Rhapsody—A major, No. 1—LP

GERSHWIN—An American in Paris—LP

GOULD—"Spirituals" for Orchestra—LP

IBERT—"Escales" (Port of Call)—LP

LISZT—Mephisto Waltz—LP

MOUSSORGSKY—Gopack—(The Fair at Sorotchinski)—LP

MOUSSORGSKY-RAVEL—Pictures at an Exhibition—LP

PROKOFIEFF—Symphony No. 5—LP

RACHMANINOFF—Concerto No. 2 in C minor for Piano and Orchestra (with Gygory Sandor, piano)

RACHMANINOFF—Symphony No. 2 in E minor

SAINT-SAENS—Concerto for Piano and Orchestra No. 4 in C minor (with Robert Casadesus)—LP

SIBELIUS—Symphony No. 4 in A minor

TSCHAIKOWSKY—Nutcracker Suite—LP

TSCHAIKOWSKY—Suite "Mozartiana"—LP

TSCHAIKOWSKY—Symphony No. 6 in B minor ("Pathétique")—LP

WAGNER—Lohengrin—Bridal Chamber Scene (Act III—Scene 2)—(with Helen Traubel, soprano, and Kurt Baum, tenor)—LP

WAGNER—Lohengrin—Elsa's Dream (Act I, Scene 2) (with Helen Traubel, soprano)

WAGNER—Siegfried Idyll—LP

WAGNER—Tristan und Isolde—Excerpts (with Helen Traubel, soprano)

WAGNER—Die Walküre—Act III (Complete) (with Helen Traubel, soprano and Herbert Janssen, baritone)—LP

WAGNER—Die Walküre—Duet (Act I, Scene 3) (with Helen Traubel, soprano and Emery Darcy, tenor)—LP

WOLF-FERRARI—"Secret of Suzanne," Overture

Under the Direction of Igor Stravinsky

STRAVINSKY—Firebird Suite—LP

STRAVINSKY—Fireworks (Feu d'Artifice)—LP

STRAVINSKY—Four Norwegian Moods

STRAVINSKY—Le Sacre du Printemps (The Consecration of the Spring)—LP

STRAVINSKY—Scènes de Ballet—LP

STRAVINSKY—Suite from "Petrouchka"—LP

STRAVINSKY—Symphony in Three Movements—LP

Under the Direction of Sir Thomas Beecham

MENDELSSOHN—Symphony No. 4, in A major ("Italian")

SIBELIUS—Melisande (from "Pelleas and Melisande")

SIBELIUS—Symphony No. 7 in C major—LP

TSCHAIKOWSKY—Capriccio Italien

Under the Direction of John Barbirolli

BACH-BARBIROLLI—Sheep May Safely Graze (from the "Birthday Cantata")—LP

BERLIOZ—Roman Carnival Overture

BRAHMS—Symphony No. 2, in D major

BRAHMS—Academic Festival Overture—LP

BRUCH—Concerto No. 1, in G minor (with Nathan Milstein, violin)—LP

DEBUSSY—First Rhapsody for Clarinet (with Benny Goodman, clarinet)

DEBUSSY—Petite Suite: Ballet

MOZART—Concerto in B-flat major (with Robert Casadesus, piano)

MOZART—Symphony No. 25 in G minor, K. 183

RAVEL—La Valse

RIMSKY-KORSAKOV—Capriccio Espagnol

SIBELIUS—Symphony No. 1, in E minor

SIBELIUS—Symphony No. 2, in D major

SMETANA—The Bartered Bride—Overture

TSCHAIKOWSKY—Theme and Variations (from Suite No. 3 in G)—LP

Under the Direction of Andre Kostelanetz

GERSHWIN—Concerto in F (with Oscar Levant)—LP

Under the Direction of Dimitri Mitropoulos

KHACHATURIAN—Concerto for Piano and Orchestra (with Oscar Levant, piano)—LP

VICTOR RECORDS

Under the Direction of Arturo Toscanini

BEETHOVEN—Symphony No. 7 in A major

BRAHMS—Variations on a Theme by Haydn

DUKAS—The Sorcerer's Apprentice

GLUCK—Orfeo ed Euridice—Dance of the Spirits

HAYDN—Symphony No. 4 in D major (The Clock)

MENDELSSOHN—Midsummer Night's Dream—Scherzo

MOZART—Symphony in D major (K. 385)

ROSSINI—Barber of Seville—Overture

ROSSINI—Semiramide—Overture

ROSSINI—Italians in Algiers—Overture

VERDI—Traviata—Preludes to Acts I and II

WAGNER—Excerpts—Lohengrin—Die Götterdämmerung—Siegfried Idyll

Under the Direction of John Barbirolli

DEBUSSY—Iberia (Images, Set 3, No. 2)

PURCELL—Suite for Strings with four Horns, two Flutes, English Horn

RESPIGHI—Fountains of Rome

RESPIGHI—Old Dances and Airs (Special recording for members of the Philharmonic-Symphony League of New York)

SCHUBERT—Symphony No. 4 in C minor (Tragic)

SCHUMANN—Concerto for Violin and Orchestra in D minor (with Yehudi Menuhin, violin)

TSCHAIKOWSKY—Francesca da Rimini—Fantasia

Under the Direction of Willem Mengelberg

J. C. BACH—Arr. Stein—Sinfonia in B-flat major

J. S. BACH—Arr. Mahler—Air for G String (from Suite for Orchestra)

BEETHOVEN—Egmont Overture

HANDEL—Alcina Suite

MENDELSSOHN—War March of the Priests (from Athalia)

MEYERBEER—Prophète—Coronation March

SAINT-SAENS—Rouet d'Omphale (Omphale's Spinning Wheel)

SCHELLING—Victory Ball

WAGNER—Flying Dutchman—Overture

WAGNER—Siegfried—Forest Murmurs (Waldweben)

www.ingramcontent.com/pod-product-compliance
Ingram Content Group UK Ltd.
Pitfield, Milton Keynes, MK11 3LW, UK
UKHW020011110225
454898UK00005B/380